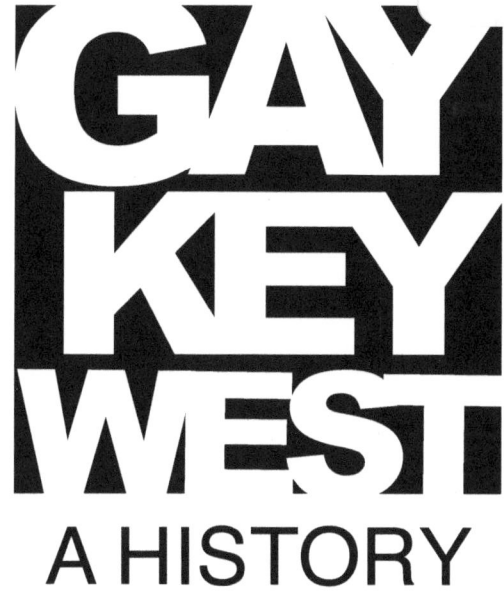

GAY KEY WEST

A HISTORY

Stories of the famous, infamous
and forgotten gay men
who transformed the island

• • • Expanded 2nd Edition • • •

Richard McGarry and Greg Madsen

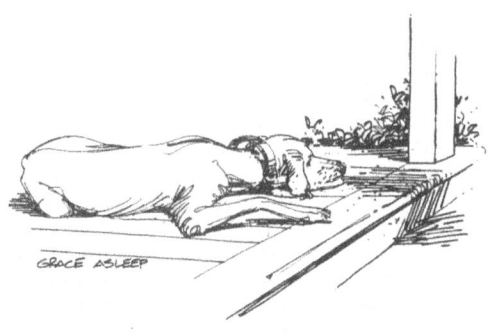

GRACE ASLEEP

Photo Credits

Florida Keys History Center of Monroe County Library - 7, 12, 13, 17, 22, 23, 37, 39, 42, 45, 46, 47, 51, 52, 57, 63, 67, 73, 75, 77
R. Kevin Mallinson - 9, 15 • Bobby Nesbitt - 18, 20
UF Special Collections - 26 • Tony Falcone - 41 • MCC Key West - 10
Key West Business Guild Archive 11,62, 74, 87, 92, 94 • La-Te-Da - 44
Andy Newman - 79 • State Library and Archives of Florida - 43
Orlando Fernandez, public domain - 52 • Library of Congress - 55
Joe Lowe - 64 • Rick Berard - 66 • Peter Arnow - 88
RNS, Reuters - 68 • AIDS Help - 70, 71 • Kenny Weschler - 72 •
Rob O"Neal - 89 • J.T. Thompson - 10, 76 • Donie Lee - 80, 81
Judith Moffett -

Acknowledgments

Thank you Kevin Mallinson for editing the final text. He found lots that needed to be fixed. Everybody we talked to said be sure to go see Tony Falcone. So we did, and he spilled more Key West stories than we could possibly fit into one book. Others who helped include June Keith, Corey Malcolm and Nancy Klingener, of the Key West Library, Flo Turcotte and Steven Hersh, of the University of Florida Special Collections Research Library, Kevin Theriault, of Key West Business Guild, and Steven Torrence, of the Metropolitan Community Church. Some of the drawings by Richard McGarry were originally published in Key West Sketchbook (1990, Maupin House).

Published by McGarry and Madsen
16822 SE 92nd Danna Avenue
The Villages, FL 32162
mcgarryandmadsen@mac.com
Distributed to the trade by Ingram Content Group
Second Edition, 2024
ISBN: 979-8-9897879-0-6
Library of Congress Control Number: 2024900665

If we don't tell our stories, someone else
might write our history.

R. Kevin Mallinson

Everything that you think is solid
is actually fleeting and ephemeral.

Joyce Carol Oates

Peg Hilmer, aunt of playwright Jimmy Kirkwood (*A Chorus Line*), sipping her cocktail on the pool deck of La Terraza De Marti, seated in front of a chorus line of La-Te-Da waiters in their bikini uniforms.

Lynn Kaufelt called Peg "Key West's favorite aunt." Jimmy built a second story apartment onto his cottage in the Conch Grove compound on Bakers Lane, and moved into it, so that she could live on the first floor below him.

The photo was taken for a La-Te-Da ad in the Founders Society's playbill for the Tennessee Williams Fine Arts Theater. They rejected the ad as too racy for their 1970s audience. The ensuing uproar was even better advertising for Larry Formica (p. 44) than the ad.

TABLE OF CONTENTS

INTRODUCTION

Our history of gay Key West begins on December 23rd, 1954. Only three months before that day, Key West Police Chief Bienvenido Perez had promised to rid the city of the "scores of sex-deviates" who had supposedly flocked to Key West to escape a crackdown by Miami police. "The town is full of them," he commented. "We don't want that kind of people in Key West." Perez also noted that there were citizen complaints that perverts were congregating in certain bars and beaches. "They are actually whistling at sailors as they walk down the street," he added. Chief Perez instructed the entire police force to jail obvious deviates "wherever and whenever they are found."

Judge Promises Crackdown On Local Perverts

But Says He Won't Condone Molesting Of Homosexuals

But on December 23rd, 1954, City Judge Enrique Esquinaldo gave a three-month jail sentence to a local hotel cook for beating a man, then taking his money, watch, and car, all because "he propositioned me," according to the defendant. The term was unusually severe for city court and the maximum under city law.

An article about the incident in the *Key West Citizen* was headlined "Judge Promises Crackdown on Local Perverts - But Says He Won't Condone Molesting of Homosexuals." It was a significant event in two ways: 1) the first time the word homosexual was used in the newspaper, and 2) the first time beating and robbing a gay man was taken seriously as a crime—which is why it was front-page news.

Things were beginning to change. Twenty-nine years later an out-and-proud homosexual, Richard Heyman, was elected mayor of Key West. But no one in 1954 would have believed it possible.

There were gay rights protests and lawsuits along the way. But the change is mostly due to the gay men who moved to the island, along with those who were born in Key West, becoming part of the fabric of the community. Over the years they have served as firemen, policemen, politicians, doctors, contractors, lawyers, shopkeepers—and, of course, trolley drivers, drag queens, bartenders, and artists.

Here are their stories.

Sailor in phone booth at La Concha Hotel, 1960s

TIMELINE

Our story of the history of Gay Key West is told through a series of biographical sketches of the gay men that made the dramatic changes happen over the years. But, to tie it all together, here are the key events in chronological order, along with links to pages with more about each one.

1954 - Key West Police Chief promises to rid the town of "scores of sex-deviates." But, later the same year, City Judge Enrique Esquinaldo sentences local man to jail for beating and robbing a gay man, saying he won't condone molesting of homosexuals. A first. (p. 6)

1961 - Jim Russell and Peter Pell buy Key West Handprint Fabrics, a small screen printing shop in Harbor House and hire Suzie Zuzek to design their fabrics. (p. 12)

1967 - David Wolkowsky opens the Pier House waterfront resort at 0 Duval Street, and invites his many gay friends in literature and the arts to come visit. It marked the beginning of the revival of the island's tourist economy. (p. 48)

1971 - First gay guest house. Ed Seebol opens "Big Ruby's," recognized as the island's first gay guest house (p. 24).

1973 - "Conch Grove" compound created on Watson Street. Designer

8

Danny Stirrup remodeled a cluster of 11 dilapidated cottages into a haven for famous and soon-to-be famous gay artists and writers. (p. 32)

1976 - First gay bathhouse steams up. Dennis Bitner opens Club Key West on Truman Avenue. (p. 28)

1975 - The Monster arrives in Key West. The legendary gay bar only lasted until 1983, but became a big draw for gay tourists of the era.

1975 - Key West Business Guild formed to promote gay tourism and support the growing community of gay-owned businesses. (p. 88)

1979 - Local Baptist preacher places anti-gay ad in Key West Citizen demanding that county commission do something about the infestation of female impersonators and queers on the island. (p. 36)

1979 - First Fantasy Fest parade down Duval Street - Created by two local gay couples, it grew over the years to become a major, week-long event. (p. 40 and 42)

1981 - Kevin Mallinson becomes first openly gay fireman in America. (p. 14)

1982 - First Key West Gay Pride Parade - down Duval Street. (p. 76)

1983 - Richard Heyman elected mayor- becoming the first openly gay mayor in the U.S. (p. 74)

1983 - International Gay and Lesbian Travel Association (IGLTA) started - by Key West travel agents, lodging, and attraction owners. (p. 84)

1983 - Key West's most famous gay resident dies - Tennessee Williams chokes to death on a swallowed pill bottle in a New York hotel. (p. 52)

1985 - First service at Metropolitan Community Church (MCC) in former Salvation Army chapel at 1215 Petronia Street. (p. 68)

1986 - AIDS Help charity started to support rising number of local gay men in health crisis. (p. 24 and 70)

1995 - Fire destroys the Copa, popular gay nightclub in 600 block of Duval Street. (p. 72)

1996 - Debut of New Year's Eve drag queen drop in red shoe at New Orleans House. (p. 89)

1997 - Key West AIDS Memorial inaugurated. (p. 83)

1998 - Domestic Partnerships become legal in Key West (p. 69)

2000 - "One Human Family" becomes official motto - of City of Key West by declaration of Mayor Jimmy Weekley (p.76)

2002 - Gay Welcome Center opened on Truman Avenue by the Key West Business Guild to serve the quarter-million gay and lesbian visitors each year. Later moved to current location at 808 Duval Street. (p. 88)

2003 - 1.25 mile long "Sea to Sea" Rainbow Flag unfurled on Duval Street by thousands of volunteers during Gay Pride Week. (p. 78)

2008 - Donie Lee becomes the city's first gay police chief.

2015 - Rainbow Crosswalks installed - spanning all four corners at Petronia and Duval Streets in gay entertainment district.

2015 - The first gay wedding in the Florida Keys - uniting two local bartenders who won a lawsuit to overturn the Florida same-sex marriage ban. (p. 68)

2015 - Lighthouse Court goes "all welcome" - dropping it's "gay male only" status. At peak in the 1980s, there were over 30 exclusively gay guest houses on the island, but only three remain. (p. 85)

LIGHTHOUSE COURT

JIM RUSSELL & PETER PELL

Key West's largest employer during the tough times of the 1960s and '70s—not counting the U.S. Navy—was Key West Handprint Fabrics, with over 150 locals on the payroll. It was owned by Jim Russell and Peter Pell, a gay couple who brought their sense of style from years on Broadway to the island. They were also old-school gay flamboyant. A former waiter at the Pier House remembers that "we all knew when Peter and Jim were in the restaurant because of their cologne."

Jim Russell

The original location of Key West Handprint Fabrics at 423 Front Street, in the Harbor House.

A big part of their success was Suzie Zuzek, another transplanted New Yorker. Suzie was a WAC (Women's Air Corps) in World War 2 and graduate of Pratt Institute, with experience in fabric design, who had married a Conch and recently moved to Key West with her husband. She told her friends up north that the place was like "Dr. Seuss Island" after she arrived, but came to love Key West's quirkiness. Suzie did hundreds of graphic, brightly-colored tropical designs for their fabrics, which became part of the company national image.

Jim and Peter's marketing talents and Suzie's designs drove the rapid growth of the company. Jim printed her designs on the sails of his personal sailboat, crewed the boat with attractive young men and women wearing outfits of their fabrics, and sent them out to welcome the cruise ships as they headed to port in the 1970s.

Their later factory and store at 529 Front Street.

They also invited tourists to "watch us print" in the silk-screen factory behind their retail store. A collaboration with women's wear designer Lilly Pulitzer ended up taking up much of their fabric production for about 15 years, although they also continured to sell their own line of clothing. They supplied Lilly with an average of 5,000 yards a week in the 1960s.

Pulitzer eventually switched to another fabric supplier and Key West Handprint's business faded in the years after Jim and Peter's death in the 1980s. But Suzie's designs are now legendary. They have been featured in exhibits by the Cooper Hewitt Museum in New York and the Key West Art and Historical Society's Custom House Museum. She is also the subject of the recent book *Suzie Zuzek for Lilly Pulitzer: The Artist Behind an Iconic Fashion Brand*.

Workers screen-printing fabrics at factory.

KEVIN MALLINSON

Kevin Mallinson never intended to be the first openly gay professional firefighter in America. But his grandparents were both in the fire service in England during World War II. He admired them and often considered following in their footsteps. So when he saw a City of Key West firefighter job listing in 1981, Kevin took the civil service test, passed, and got hired.

Being gay was not a problem in his previous jobs around the island. So he didn't think the new one would be much different. But when he arrived at the fire station on his first day, the other firemen stood around him, staring and eerily quiet, until one of them leaned in and said "We heard you're a faggot. We heard you're a god-damned faggot!"

With that, he began a four-year odyssey, enduring anti-gay slurs, inappropriate sexual innuendos, social ostracism, and sabotage. Kevin passed the required fire college boot camp at the top of his class when other Key West new recruits failed, and became a permanent employee. Yet the homophobic atmosphere in the fire station never really changed.

Kevin wrote a memoir about his Key West firehouse years entitled *Alarm in the Firehouse*. It covers the problems he encountered and how he dealt with them, but also explains the day-to-day workings of a fire station, what life was like in Key West in the 1980s, and the beginning of the AIDS crisis that consumed Key West back then.

Kevin eventually decided that nursing was his true calling, quit the fire department, got a 2-year degree at Florida Keys Community College, and continued his education to the PhD level over the following years, specializing in HIV care and research. He recently retired as an Associate Professor of Nursing at George Mason University. Kevin and his husband now split their time between Washington, DC, and Lewes, Delaware.

State Archives of Florida

Kevin at the nozzle during a controlled burn.

JAMES LEO HERLIHY

"The flowers, the air, the smell of the sea, my youth. We were terrific together." That's how author James Leo Herlihy remembered Key West during his years on the island in the 1960s.

Also, Tennessee Williams became a good friend and mentor. For a while, they met each summer day at twilight for a swim in the ocean. "It was inexpressibly comforting to have the daily company of a kindred spirit," he told one interviewer. "Just knowing we were involved in the same lunatic pursuit provided some essential ground that meant everything to me."

Herlihy was most famous for his novel, and later movie, *Midnight Cowboy*. It, and most of his other books like *Season of the Witch* and *All Fall Down,* are about people hanging on at the edge of American society. As a gay man, he understood.

"None of us feels that he's entirely normal," he once wrote. "We're all moving along hoping we're getting away with an image of normality—but our secret is that we've got this sweet little place that isn't quite like anybody else's."

Jim loved that the counter-culture had its own world in Old Town back then, and his cottage in Conch Grove became a party spot and safe-house for his hippie friends.

Unfortunately, as Herlihy became a celebrity, with a string of best-sellers and movie contracts, he could no longer be the anonymous Key West free-spirit he once was. So he departed. Jim wrote some of his best work while on the island and, although he continued to write afterwards, he never published anything more after leaving Key West.

✦ ✦ ✦ ✦ ✦

Las Palmas del Mundo, at the corner of Southard and Frances, was an authentic hippie restaurant of the 1970s. Their specialty was strange and delicious varieties of fresh-caught fish served in a lush, overgrown tropical garden. The owner/chef was Gail Brockway. It was featured in *Vogue* magazine as the best restaurant in Key West and had lines out the door most nights.

BOBBY NESBITT

It was 1976 and Bobby Nesbitt wanted to get out of New York. He loved his time in Key West on a recent vacation, so the island felt like a good place for a fresh start.

And it was a good decision. Bobby is an accomplished pianist and singer, specializing in the Great American Songbook. There were plenty of piano bars around town, and he was immediately popular. Rent was $125 a month for an apartment on Olivia Street. Living was cheap. But then so was the $5/hour pay.

Those magic moments that many who have lived in Key West like to tell about happened pretty quickly. First, while he was playing at the Monster bar in 1979, Leonard Bernstein walked in and sat down next to him on the piano bench. "Someone said I should come and listen to you," he said. "Play something for me."

Bernstein liked what he heard and became a regular, sitting at the piano with Bobby and playing songs from "West Side Story" while Bobby sang along.

He also met Tennessee Williams while playing piano bar. Bobby remembers asking if he could play something for him. "Sugar, I don't care what you play as long as it's sad," he said.

Later, Bernstein and Tennessee showed up together. They sat on either side of him, playing and singing show tunes for hours.

Then, shortly afterward, he met Mike Mulligan, the love of his life, and they have been together ever since.

Life was good and, as his fame spread, Bobby got more prestigious gigs like the Fairmont Hotel in San Francisco, and cabarets in Europe. He also started doing concerts playing only the works of a single composer, mixing in stories about the composer and history of each song.

Bobby officially retired from performing in 2021, but he still occasionally performs for special events at the Tennessee Williams Theater and the Harry Truman Little White House.

Just don't ask him to play "Piano Man."

❖ ❖ ❖ ❖ ❖ ❖ ❖

LARRY HARVEY

"Larry Harvey was the greatest entertainer that Key West has ever known—and you can quote me on that," according to Bobby Nesbitt. "I always said he made Ethel Merman sound timid! He was also kind and supportive. I would never have had the success I had without him."

Larry was working the lounge at the Ramada Inn on North Roosevelt to a full house every night when Bobby first started playing there in 1976.

He seemed be everywhere during the 1970s and '80s, lending his voice to church concerts, local theater productions, and special occasions for his friends. And he was the first choice for a singing Santa Claus at Christmas parties. Women loved to get photographed sitting on Santa's knee.

Larry also had a day job for 30 years as a tour guide at the Hemingway House. His tour commentary was known to be a little flamboyant. For example, he liked to instruct tour guests "Now swoop through these doors like Loretta Young..."

He had a life-long relationship with Alan Ferguson, and died in 2012 at the age of 92. Those who knew Larry remember "a most beloved man."

DON PINDER

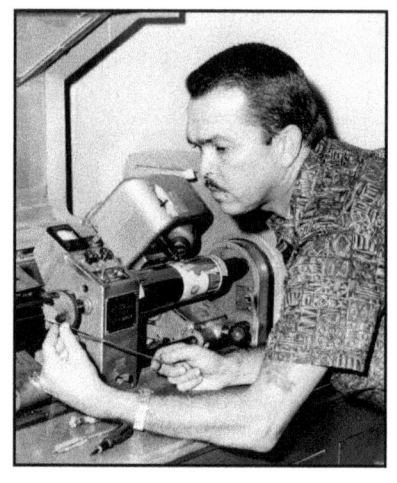

Don Pinder was a native Conch and gruff ex-Marine with a crew-cut and tattoos. He was the only staff photographer for the *Key West Citizen* for 35 years, starting in the early 1950s.

But there was another side of him that was not so well-known due to the era he lived in: Don was also gay and a close friend of Tennessee Williams.

There were no gay bars in the 1950s when he and Tennessee first met. But there were certain places in town where gay men would hang out, like the Bamboo Room on Appelrouth Lane and the Tradewinds at the corner of Caroline and Duval. They saw each other often at these get-togethers, and Don also visited him in this home. He remembers listening to dialogue for new plays being tried out in Tennessee's living room.

Williams was shy and not too talkative back then, according to Don. He preferred that his "companion and secretary" Frank Merlo keep the conversation going.

Don began photographing Tennessee, almost daily for awhile, as a personal project. But the scotch and tranquilizers changed him over the years, and eventually Don dropped out of his social circle.

Pinder published a book in 1983 entitled *Offbeat Key West,* with a collection of his favorite photos. It is long out-of-print and an expensive collectible.

He also donated his extensive photo collection of day-to-day life in Key West to the Florida Keys History Center at the Key West Library shortly before he died. The History Center published 1,571 of his best images online at https://www.flickr.com/photos/keyslibraries/albums/.

Bamboo Room at 422 Appelrouth Lane, just off Duval Street, circa 1965.

ED SEEBOL

Ed Seebol walked away from an IBM computer sales career in New York City in 1970 and headed for what he intended to be semi-retirement in Key West. After settling in, he bought an old two-story Conch house at the corner of Whitehead Street and Aronovitz Lane, and remodeled it into Key West's first gay guesthouse.

The rooms were small and the bathroom was down the hall, but for less than $100 you could spend a whole week at "Big Ruby's" in Key West. A three-line classified ad in *After Dark* (a gay New York arts and entertainment magazine) at $1 per word was enough to fill the house much of the year.

Then, in 1978, Ed bought a bigger place a few blocks away on Appelrouth Lane, just off Duval, and moved his guesthouse operation there. Cal Culver (the porn star known as Casey Donovan) bought the old location and changed the name to Casa Donovan. But that's a whole other story on page 30.

The AIDS epidemic hit Key West especially hard in the mid-1980s, and the rapidly growing number of local AIDS patients urgently needed physical and financial assistance. So Ed organized "AIDS Help" on his back porch with a few friends in 1986 to meet the need. Then he became Executive Director as the organization grew from a dozen volunteers to a full-time staff of 14, about 150 volunteers, and a million-dollar budget.

Ed left AIDS Help and Key West for California in 1993, likely due to burn-out from the stress of running the organization during its very difficult first eight years. But, before departing, he gave gay Key West one more gift.

He and his partner had wanted to adopt a child, preferably an "unadoptable" boy with physical or mental disabilities. But State of Florida law forbade adoption by gays or lesbians. Seebol sued the state on the grounds that it was unconstitutional and won, clearing the way for gay adoptions throughout Florida.

Today, the bright yellow "Seebol Place" housing complex at 711 Catherine Street that provides small apartments for the formerly homeless has been named in his honor. However, the small plaque at the front of the building does not even list his full name, much less his accomplishments, and is dedicated instead to a local business. Other than that, Key West's first gay guesthouse owner, founder and first executive director of AIDS Help, and gay rights activist is largely forgotten.

ERNIE MICKLER

Ernie Mickler (pronounced mike-ler) had been in Key West for several years, working as a houseman at Oasis Guesthouse on Fleming Street, when he got the phone call. The book he had been working on for more than a decade was finally accepted by a publisher. It would have been in print sooner, but the title he insisted on using triggered numerous rejection letters: *White Trash Cooking*.

Ernie liked to explain the distinction between "White Trash" capitalized and "white trash" in lower case. "Manners and pride" made the difference according to Ernie. He was proud to have been raised poor and White Trash in Palm Valley, Florida, just south of Jacksonville Beach.

Ernie had already been testing out recipes from his collection, like Mock Cooter Soup and Our Lord's Scripture Cake, by hosting White Trash dinner parties at gay guest houses around Old Town. If you got a half-dozen or more gay men together, he would come to the house and cook and serve a White Trash menu, while regaling everyone with stories and photos of the folkways and oddities of the little rural community where he grew up. It was also a way for him to make some extra money.

The book was a phenomenon, rising quickly up the *New York Times* best-seller list in 1986. The royalties enabled him to buy a house in Moccasin Branch, a small settlement near where he grew up. Ernie followed up two years later with

Sinkin Spells, Hot Flashes, Fits and Cravins. Both books are admired today as much for the photos and stories about Southern life at the bottom rung of the economic ladder as for their recipes.

One of Ernie's long-time friends insists that, if it wasn't for Key West, it all would have never happened. The island was the right place for his talent to blossom.

Ernie died from HIV complications on November 15th, 1988, one day after *Sinkin' Spells* was published. His original manuscripts, photos, and personal papers are now archived in the University of Florida's Special Area Studies Collection at the George A. Smathers Library, in Gainesville.

DENNIS BITNER

The name Dennis Bitner is engraved on the historic marker at the corner of Wall and Fitzpatrick Streets that commemorates the mock secession of Key West from the United States in the spring of 1982. He was one of the six founding fathers of what became the "Conch Republic."

If you don't already know about this bit of Key West history, it was in response to a U.S. Border Patrol roadblock of U.S. 1 (the only road into and out of the Keys) near the Last Chance Saloon in Florida City. Vehicles were searched for narcotics and illegal immigrants, and proof of citizenship was required before passing.

Some days the traffic was backed up for hours. This was a disaster for tourism, and complaints by local business owners were ignored. As Key West Mayor Dennis Wardlow pointed out, they were treating Key West like a foreign country.

So a group of concerned businessmen, including our Dennis, decided that maybe Key West should just go ahead and become a foreign country, if only symbolicly. Mayor Wardlow and the city commission proclaimed Key West's independence on April 23rd, 1982, and the mayor was made prime minister of the new republic. He immediately declared war against the United States, by symbolically breaking a loaf of stale Cuban bread over the head of a man dressed in a naval uniform. Then, after a minute, Wardlow surrendered to the uniformed man and applied for one billion dollars in foreign aid.

Needless to say, the publicity stunt got a lot of national press and the blockade was lifted shortly afterward. Conch Independence Days is now an annual celebration.

Dennis was the owner of Club Key West, part of the national gay bathhouse chain. He was also one of the founders of the Monroe County Tourist Development Council. The AIDS epidemic a few years later sent his business into a nosedive and Club Key West closed. The location, at 611 Truman Avenue, is now Truman Hotel.

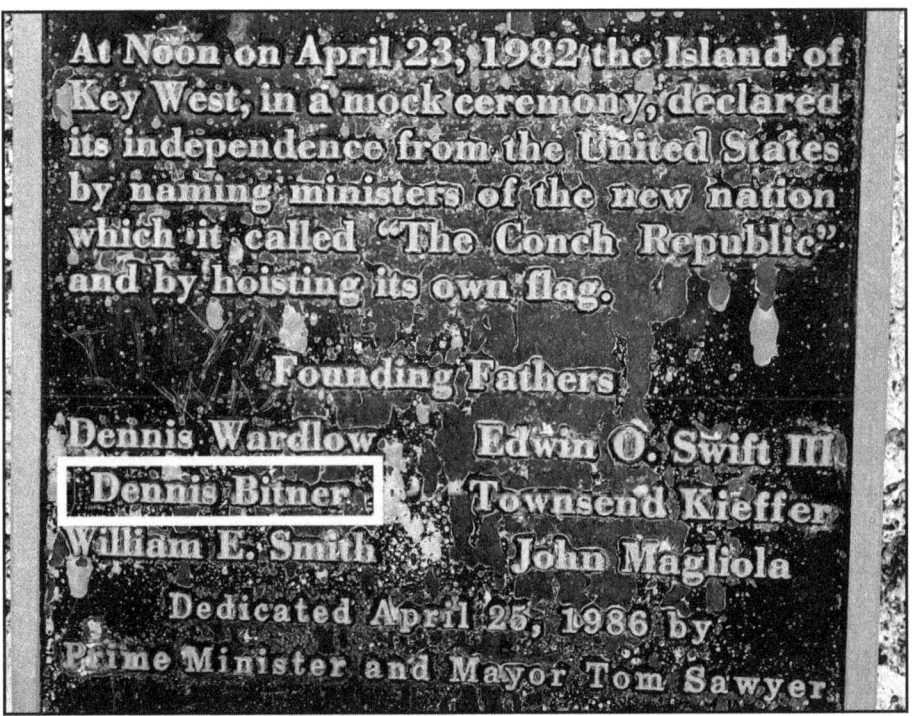

CAL CULVER

Becoming a gay porn star was easy for Cal Culver, better known by his stage name Casey Donovan. He had all the right equipment and a dazzling smile. His starring role in the landmark gay movie *Boys in the Sand* was a sensation in 1971.

But what he really wanted was to cross over into mainstream movies. Unfortunately, Cal's notoriety as a porn star nixed those dreams. Unless you count a couple of straight sexploitation films and off-Broadway plays.

Casa Donovan is a law office today.

After the breakup of his four-year affair with the actor/writer Tom Tryon, Cal decided to move to Key West and reinvent himself. He bought the two-story Conch house on the corner of Whitehead Street and Aronovitz Lane in 1978 that was formerly Big Ruby's guesthouse. Cal renamed it Casa Donovan, and became a bed-and-breakfast host. He loved to show his guests the large framed photo montage at the top of the stairs of himself and each of his Phi Sigma Epsilon fraternity brothers from this college days back in New York.

But he struggled to keep the business going, and it eventually failed. Roger Edmondson, author of a biography of Cal entitled *Boys In The Sand: Casey Donovan, All-American Sex Star*, called Casa Donovan "the money pit that devoured almost every penny he made." Cal ended up both waiting tables at Tux restaurant (now Margaritaville) on Duval Street and hustling for a while before leaving town.

His porn fame enabled him to become a high-priced escort/prostitute and he also drifted back into porn. Cal's last movie role, shortly before his death in 1987 from an HIV-related infection, was in the Christopher Rage film *Fucked Up*. If you are familiar with Christopher Rage movies, you know they are not for the squeamish. He was brutally fisted while very high.

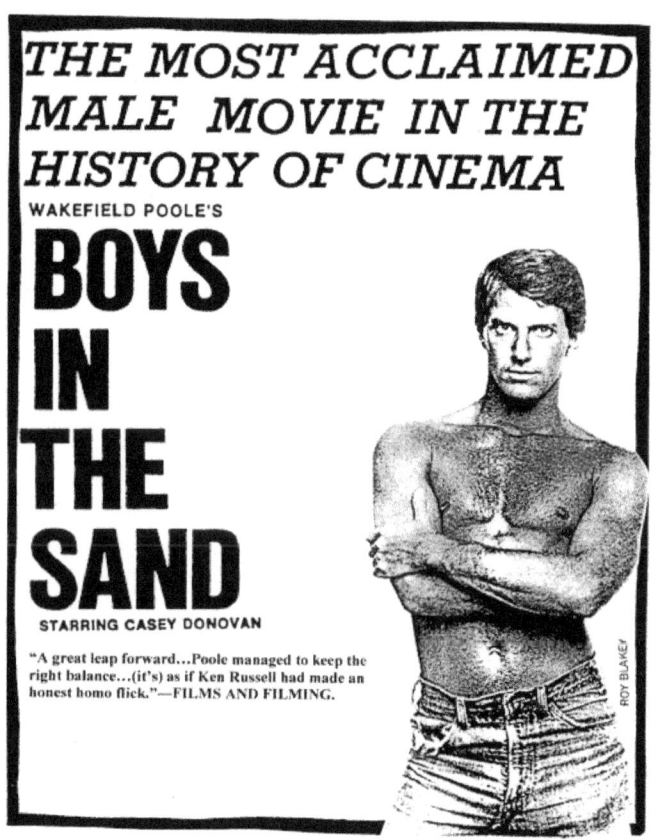

THE MOST ACCLAIMED MALE MOVIE IN THE HISTORY OF CINEMA

WAKEFIELD POOLE'S

BOYS IN THE SAND

STARRING CASEY DONOVAN

"A great leap forward...Poole managed to keep the right balance...(it's) as if Ken Russell had made an honest homo flick."—FILMS AND FILMING.

ROY BLAKEY

DAN STIRRUP

Dan Stirrup, a talented and flamboyant teenager, was in both the band and chorus in the 1940s at Key West High. In his senior year he was a member of an all-male quartet that called themselves the Rebels of Satire, singing and dancing a humorous, swing version of Stephen Foster's "Suwannee River" in a Junior Women's Club cabaret show.

He later became a well-known local architectural designer. One of his creations is the "Polynesian House" at 1415 Alberta Street. Its soaring roof is a familiar landmark and was featured in *Architectural Digest* in 1968.

In the early 1970s Danny bought and remodeled a cluster of eleven dilapidated cigar-maker cottages on Watson Street, added a pool, lush landscaping and fencing, and named it "Conch Grove." The compound became the home of famous gay writers like James Leo Herlihy (*Midnight Cowboy*) and James Kirkwood (*A Chorus Line*), along with local gay professionals like Jack Phillips and Joe Trice, of Phillips and Trice Surveyors.

Novelist David Kaufelt (*Six Months with an Older Woman*) and his family also lived there for several years. His wife Lynn featured it in her book *Key West Writers and Their Houses*. She noted that their house was "imbued with atmosphere, with ghosts, with traditions, with life."

The Polynesian House as it looks today.

Danny became a hero in 1953 when he and another local man heard the hysterical screams of a young Navy wife who was being attacked by a rapist in a Fleming Street apartment. They captured him on Elizabeth Street after a "wild chase and battle," according to the *Key West Citizen*.

GEORGE FIELDER

George Fielder was a middle-aged high school art teacher in Miami when his mother died in 1975 and left him a small inheritance. He loved Key West and his big dream was to open an art gallery on the island someday. The inheritance wasn't a lot, but it was enough to move to Key West and begin living his dream.

The photo of him at right is from a Miami Senior High School yearbook just before he moved to Key West, ditched the tie, grew a beard, and started smiling.

George rented the entire upstairs of Guild Hall at 614 Duval Street for $140 a month and opened the Wild Wind Gallery. The name came from the 1940s novel *Reap The Wild Wind* by Thelma Strabel, which was made into a Cecile B. DeMille adventure/romance movie extravaganza set in the Keys. The film featured the obligatory hurricane, shipwreck, giant octopus, and John Wayne.

George made friends easily in the local arts community and enjoyed happy hour most afternoons at Delmonicos a few blocks down Duval Street. His themed and carefully curated art shows were featured regularly in the *Key West Citizen* and he hosted monthly poetry readings and piano recitals at the gallery. Life was good.

But the gallery only made money during the four-month winter tourist season and lost money the rest of the year. His inheritance ran out after two years and he headed back to Miami and his old teaching job.

Did he regret the Key West sabbatical? No, not according to George. Like many before and after him, it made wonderful memories and was worth it all.

MORRIS WRIGHT

As more and more gay men visited Key West in 1970s, and then moved there, some locals became distressed. The gays brought money. That was good. They also purchased real estate, especially in the distressed Old Town area. But they were "different," and the more effeminate gay men saw Key West as a haven where they could just be themselves, and not have to "butch it up" like back home.

A growing contingent of Conchs got upset. They felt their island was being taken over by the "queers." And the leader of the charge to fix the perceived problem was Reverend Morris Wright. Morris was not gay, but his story is included here because of his impact on gay life in Key West at the time.

Wright was the pastor of a fundamentalist Baptist church on adjacent Stock Island. Morris saw the influx of gays as an opportunity to embellish his status as a tough, fire-and-brimstone preacher.

So, on January 12, 1979, he placed a large ad in the *Key West Citizen* demanding that the County Commission "help bring back some of the uniqueness of the Key West and the Florida Keys way of life." And this is how he proposed to accomplish that: "If I were the chief of police, I would get me a hundred good men, give them each a baseball bat and have them walk down Duval Street and dare one of these freaks to stick his head over the edge of the sidewalk. That is the way it was done in Key West in the days I remember and loved. Female impersonators and queers were loaded into a deputy's automobile and shipped to the county line."

After he published his screed, the attacks on gay men increased for a while, especially by Conch teenagers.

Reverend Wright essentially gave them permission to beat up anyone that looked queer.

Also, he became an easy source of a quotable opposing opinion for any reporter writing an upbeat article about the happenings in gay Key West. Shortly before the third annual Fantasy Fest parade in 1981, he told a United Press reporter that "We consider Fantasy Fest nothing more than a revival of demonism. Fantasy Fest is ungodly, indecent and immoral."

By that time, the parade promoters just laughed. They were delighted by the free national publicity.

✦ ✦ ✦ ✦ ✦

Rainy day on the 500 block of Duval Street in1966.

REX BRUMGART

Rex Brumgart was a Conch Train driver from the 1940s through the '60s, back when it was a small and more casually run business. Although the drivers had a script they followed, adlibbing a little and responding to what was happening on the street as the train passed was allowed.

Rex took that to an extreme. When he saw a gay man he knew as they passed, he would call out to him something like "Hi honey! Folks, that's Fred Cole. He's island royalty. Everybody wave and say hi to Fred..." And that was for his friends. He was known to slip off the route to stop the train in front of the house of a queen he disliked, and make catty comments about him over the loudspeaker, followed by his cackling laugh, before moving on. Rex somewhat resembled Truman Capote and had a similar persona, which enabled him to get away with being a prankster.

Lee Dodé tells this story about him in his book *Cruisin' Duval*: "One summer afternoon around four, two guys decided to invite 20 men over for an impromptu cocktail party in their home. Rex was not invited because the hosts knew he was working. Rex pulled a full train load of tourists to the front of the house and announced 'Ladies and gentlemen. We are going to see a typical Key West party. We'll walk through the house. Please do not order a drink, eat the hors d'oeuvres, or talk to the guests.' Thirty strangers walked through the house as the astonished guests froze, and they went out the back door onto the Conch Train and continued their trip. The hosts could only laugh once the invasion was finished."

But Rex's big claim to fame is that he started the nightly sunset celebration at Mallory Square Dock back in 1949. It was just him at first. He packed the ingredients for a few martinis and some snacks in a small carry-all, along with a beach chair and folding table. Then he lugged it all down to the dock—which was not the concrete expanse it is today, but rotting wood planks where shrimp boats docked.

Rex recalled that the sunset was so spectacular the first time that he stood up from his beach chair, lifted his martini, and shouted "Bravo!" Several amused fisherman nearby joined in.

Rex Brumgart, in the driver's seat, and Miami Mayor Robert King High smiling for the camera in the 1960s

Then he invited a few friends along, but only on Sundays at first. They traded local gossip and sipped their drinks while watching the slowly shifting kaleidoscope of colors. According to Rex, "I took the late Tennessee Williams to see his first sunset at Mallory Dock. As the last of the sun dipped below the horizon he applauded and shouted, 'Author, author! Who wrote this great play?'" Remember, they were having martinis.

By the 1970s, it became a well-known daily event, albeit without the cocktails, and often attended by hundreds of people. Local shopkeepers would close up and hang a sign on their door "GONE TO SUNSET. BACK SOON." Because sunset was also a social event, and it's hard to turn down a "you wanna get high?" invitation, "back soon" was sometimes later than you might expect.

Sunset is now bigger than ever, a must-see for island visitors, and has morphed into a carnival atmosphere next to the nightly ritual of "putting the sun to bed." Thank you Rex.

TONY FALCONE & BILL CONKLE

Tony Falcone and his partner Bill Conkle opened Fast Buck Freddies department store on Duval Street in 1976. It quickly became an island favorite for nearly 40 years. Everybody, locals and tourists alike, went to Fast Bucks, and their window displays were legendary.

Tony and "Gonzo," their rescue dog and store mascot.

Tony and Bill were also half of the foursome that created the first Fantasy Fest parade in 1979. The other couple was Frank Romano and Joe Liszka of Key West Aloe. They conceived the parade as a way to enliven October, the slowest month of the year for tourism. It's now a famous weeklong event, with the town booked to capacity.

But Fast Bucks almost didn't happen because of an incident on New Year's Eve 1975. Old Town was largely abandoned by the local Conchs at that time, but hippies and gays had flocked to the area. In the eyes of the police, both were lumped together as undesirables. Captain Tony's bar was full of partiers that night—mostly hippies, gays, and shrimpers—as the countdown to midnight began.

Then the Key West Police showed up, backed by a fire truck, and started yelling for everyone to leave. For no good reason. Those present that night were pretty sure the police were drunker than the partiers, which was not unusual for Key West. Captain Tony tried talking to the cops to defuse the situation, but then they turned a firehose on the crowd, even through the open doors of the bar.

Everybody ran, soaked, down the street and many ended up at Delmonicos bar. The police, determined to ruin the party, showed up again and tried to break it up there. Fortunately, Hilario "Charlie" Ramos came out from the back of the bar, and had a few quiet words with them. Charlie is from the wealthy Conch family that owned the local wholesale liquor distributorship and the Southernmost House, he was a former state representative for Key West, and he was gay. Finally, the seige was over.

Drawing by Ann Irvine of their original store at the corner of Duval and Appelrouth Lane.

After all the drama, Tony was not so sure about starting a business on the island. But his partner Bill just laughed it off and the rest is Key West history.

L to R, Bill Conkle, Rex Brumgart, and Tony Falcone.

FRANK ROMANO & JOE LISZKA

Frank Romano and Joe Liszka launched the Key West Fragrance And Cosmetic Factory in 1971 in the building at 540 Greene Street. Frank was the one with the nose, a master perfumer. Their first products were mainly fragrances, like 1000 Portholes ("The Original Key Lime Fragrance") and the more provocatively named Sexy Afternoon and Forbidden Gardenia. Frank and Joe formulated and bottled their cosmetic products in their small factory at the back of the store with a staff of mostly gay men.

They changed the company name to the much simpler Key West Aloe after their sunburn cream with aloe vera became popular. Although the juice from the leaves of the aloe vera plant was well known to local Conchs as a soothing home remedy for a bad sunburn, they were one of the first

Frank Romano (left) and Joe Liszka holding the plant that made their fortune.

companies to introduce aloe-based skin products to a national market.

The success of their line of aloe products enabled them to launch a national mail order business with lavish color catalogs. Frank and Joe were master marketers, but they enjoyed a good prank now and then. One of their catalogs featured a local drag queen as a model in their product photography. The makeup and lighting was so good that it would be difficult for most people to recognize anything was amiss.

Their accomplishments were many. Frank served as president of the Chamber of Commerce and was on many local boards. He and Joe were the Key West boosters that pushed to create the Tourist Development Council, which uses a tax on hotel rooms to promote the Keys as a tourist destination. Also, along with Tony and Bill of Fast Buck Freddies, they conceived the fabulously successful annual Fantasy Fest Parade that has grown to a week-long event.

But not everybody on the island loved them. Larry Formica, for example, was not amused when they named a new perfume La-Te-Da, and sued for copyright infringement.

After Frank died in 2011, Joe arranged for a fountain to be installed in the pond at the intersection at the edge of Old Town where North Roosevelt Boulevard changes to Truman Avenue, with a commemorative plaque at the sidewalk to honor his life and their accomplishments.

LARRY FORMICA

Kim Romano, niece of Frank Romano of Key West Aloe fame, once described having lunch with her grandmother on the deck at La Terraza De Marti when a "very hot" postman named John Coley arrived, put down his mail bag, ripped off his uniform and jumped naked into the pool. It was his daily habit. But next to all the topless sunbathers, it probably wasn't all that shocking for her grandma.

La-Te-Da, as it is often called, was the creation of Larry Formica. Larry was a high-energy guy, and best-known for hosting outrageous theme parties that are still talked about today.

La-Te-Da before Larry got his hands on it.

His place began in 1977 as a modest gay guesthouse occupying a home that had a history. Jose Marti had once given impassioned speeches promoting Cuban independence from its front balcony (terraza). Larry added more rooms, a restaurant, pool, large deck, plus outdoor and indoor bars, and made it Key West Fabulous. Pink tablecloths and napkins, crystal glassware, topless sunbathing by the pool, and waiters in bikinis during the day. Formal dining and a gourmet menu in the evening. The Sunday afternoon Tea Dance was famous and packed.

Although La-Te-Da was in-your-face gay, many of the customers were local heterosexuals who found it all entertaining. Unfortunately, Larry knew how to do fabulous but he was not as good at keeping the place profitable, and his ownership came to an end.

Things have changed a lot in Key West in the thirty years since he departed, but his baby is still at 1125 Duval Street, still an upscale resort, and Sunday Tea Dance lives on, bigger than ever.

FRANK FONTIS

Frank Fontis was a big, loud, macho guy and, in the tradition of Key West characters, he liked to occasionally show up at parties in full drag. He was a landscaper. Plus, Frank owned the "Old Coffee Mill and Florida Railroad Museum" at 201 Ann Street. It was more of a rinky-dink tourist trap than a real museum and he lived in back. The building's most recent occupant is Shots & Giggles bar.

Frank was also Tennessee Williams' gardener and caretaker for his house on Duncan Street when he was out of town. They were friends, although Tennessee claimed that Frank had a "genuine demonic presence" and "evil powers."

He had a fondness for young drifters and hustlers and, according to local stories, sometimes refused to pay them. Fontis was found on his front porch, nude, in a pool of blood with a gunshot hole

Frank (left) and "Tiny," planting palm trees on Front Street in 1965. Tiny was actually the opposite of tiny, and also a bouncer at local bars. According to Gordon Ross, "Tiny knew everybody."

through his head, on the morning of January 5th, 1979. Crumpled dollar bills were scattered around him.

Two young drifters were later arrested. One of them had reportedly been seen wearing Frank's heart necklace with a diamond-studded "F". But the evidence was circumstantial and both were eventually acquitted.

Monroe County Sheriff Bobby Brown in his leisure suit, showing off a truckload of fresh-caught square grouper, circa 1970s.

DAVID WOLKOWSKY

They called him "Mr. Key West." David Wolkowsky was born on the island in 1919, but hard times and the aftermath of a Cat 4 hurricane forced his family to move north to Miami just a few years later. He returned in the 1960s when he inherited a collection of dilapidated buildings in Old Town after his father died. David had been a successful redeveloper of historic properties in Philadelphia, and decided to do the same thing on the island.

Key West in the 1960s was hit by hard times. The Navy had slashed its presence on the island, leading to economic depression. Old Town storefronts were mostly empty and boarded-up. As Merili McCoy, wife of Key West's mayor, said, "a good girl would not be seen on Duval Street after dark."

But David saw the island's potential in the squalor, and built the Pier House, the island's first modern resort hotel. Then he proceeded to invite his artistic and literary friends to come visit. Meanwhile, the Chart Room bar at this new resort became a legendary hangout. Jimmy

Buffet sang there for drinks at the start of his career. Truman Capote liked the place so much he stayed for six months and wrote much of his novel *Answered Prayers* in David's trailer on the waterfront. Tennessee Williams was a close friend, and David collected his paintings.

He and his hotel are acknowledged today as the spark that ignited the transition of Key West into a world-class resort. David's sense of style permeated all of his projects, including "Ballast Key," the private island retreat seven miles off Key West where he entertained friends in later years.

He also befriended and mentored young gay entrepreneurs on the island like Tom Schmidt (Rooftop Cafe), and Tony Falcone and Bill Conkle (Fast Buck Freddies).

David died in 2018 at 99. Anyone who spent time with him has stories to tell about his wit, quirky ways, and sly charm.

Sailing by the Pier House

View of the Pier House from the water in 1980s. It was designed by Coconut Grove architect Yiannis Antoniadis. One critic called the resort "the most unusual motel design in America."

TRUMAN CAPOTE

Truman Capote never actually lived in Key West, but he visited often, especially to spend time with his friend Tennessee Williams. One of his longer stays was at the newly-built Pier House resort. Truman had rented a suite at the hotel but decided he liked the owner David Wolkowsky's seaside personal trailer better. Somehow he convinced the usually implacable David into switching living accommodations while he was there for six months. They became friends, and Truman ended up giving David the section of the original manuscript for the novel *Answered Prayers* that he was working on while there.

An oft-told story about Truman during his Pier House stay began with him having dinner with friends at a local restaurant. A table of three couples was nearby, and it became obvious that they were staring at Truman.

He told his friends to watch, because soon one of them would be coming over. And he was right. A few minutes later a woman from the table walked over with her menu and asked him to sign it, which he graciously did.

After she returned to her group, her husband became visibly upset. He stormed over to Capote's table and asked "Are you Truman Capote?" To which Truman responded in his high-pitched nasal voice, "I was this morning."

At that, the man unzipped his pants and pulled out his cock. After cradling it in the palm of his hand, he said "Can you put your signature on this."

Truman looked down at his cock, then up again at him, and said, "I don't know about my signature, but I can initial it."

L to R, Tom McGuane, Truman Capote, Tennessee Williams, and Jimmy Kirkwood at a wrap party for the film adaptation of McGuane's novel *Ninety-Two In The Shade*, shot in Key West in 1975.

Unfortunately, *Answered Prayers* was a thinly disguised tell-all about a group of wealthy, powerful women that he had charmed into telling him many of their embarrassing secrets over the years—assuming they were confidential. He called them "my swans."

When a chapter from the forthcoming, but still incomplete, book was published in *Esquire* magazine in November, 1975, it was easy for those in-the-know to figure out who each of the characters actually was. One of the socialites to which he was particularly cruel, Ann Woodward, committed suicide shortly afterward. The proverbial fecal pellets hit the fan and he was quickly banished from the elite social circles he had so diligently cultivated. The novel was never finished and his life spiraled downward from there.

TENNESSEE WILLIAMS

One of the authors, Richard McGarry, spent an afternoon visiting Tennessee Williams in 1976. He was invited by a local bon-vivant, Liz Lear. She had jumped up in his lap on a speaker box at the back of a crowded Jimmy Buffet concert in Key West the night before. Liz said simply "Mind if I sit in your lap?" just before she wiggled into place. She was part of Williams' Key West entourage and explained that "Tennessee will like you. Meet me at his house on Duncan Street tomorrow at 2."

The scene the next afternoon, like so many in Williams' life, was like something out of one of his plays. A cluster of friends and a reporter for the *Miami Herald* sat in an informal circle of chairs around the playwright. His sister Rose, who lived nearby at the time, was wearing a white dress with a pattern of huge black cabbage roses. She had undergone a lobotomy at age 23 due to schizophrenia. Rose paced slowly back and forth across the room, about eight feet each way, just off to the side of the group.

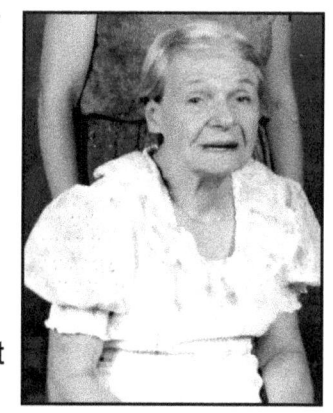

Occasionally, Tennessee would say something like "Isn't that true Rose?" and she would respond with a soft word or two while continuing to look straight ahead and pacing. There was a mayonnaise-size brown glass jar of ominous looking capsules on the kitchen counter, and Williams was noticeably inebriated.

The reporter was doing a story about him for the Herald's Sunday *Tropic* magazine and asked the typical questions for a famous playwright, including "By the way, do you have any travel plans in the near future?" To which Tennessee replied, "Yes, we will be on a lovely Mediterranean cruise in a few weeks."

That bit of information seemed insignificant until the reporter asked if he was still doing oil paintings, and Williams pointed across the room to a freshly completed canvas. It was a beach scene, with an ocean liner sinking into the waves near the horizon and a muscular, well-endowed and naked man walking out of the water onto the beach in the foreground. Small stick-on gold letters, like were once used to put a title on a composition notebook, were pushed into the paint more or less at random.

It was a memorable afternoon, but not that unusual. Anyone who has spent time in his presence in Key West has a story to tell about it.

Tennessee bought his house at 1431 Duncan Street in 1950. He also traveled extensively throughout his life and was sometimes only there sporadically. But it was his

Tennessee Williams House

home base and emotional anchor until his death from choking on a swallowed pill bottle cap in 1983 in a New York hotel.

"Baby, don't you ever forget, when you walk out that door, you're the cocksucker who just left the room."

-Tennessee Williams' admonishment to a star-struck young friend upon leaving a Hollywood celebrities party together in the 1960s.

FRANK MERLO

Tennessee Williams first met Frank Merlo on the back deck of the Atlantic House bar in Provincetown in 1948. Frank was leaning against the railing, smoking, with his back to him. Tennessee remembers that he was wearing Levis. He stared at Frank so intensely that "it must have burned a hole through his shoulder," until he turned around and smiled at him.

Williams didn't remember what his pickup line was, but a few minutes later they were in his Pontiac convertible heading for the dunes. Being obtuse about exactly what happened next, as was appropriate for the era, he noted only that he spent a fantastic hour in the dunes devoutly worshipping "the little god," although dune sand was not the best surface for it.

And so began an intense relationship, with plenty of Tennessee-style drama. It lasted for 15 years. Although open about their relationship within their social circle, they were publicly discreet. Frank was referred to as Williams' "production assistant" or sometimes "companion and secretary." And, actually, he was on a salary and took care of coordinating his travels, housekeeping, and social schedule.

But one memorable exception to Tennessee and Merlo's denial of their relationship occurred when Tennessee was in Hollywood negotiating the film rights for *A Streetcar Named Desire* with Louis B. Mayer. The movie mogul became increasingly annoyed by Frank's presence and participation in the talks. Finally, he turned to him and said, "So what *is it* that you do?" Frank replied simply, "I sleep with Mr. Williams."

Although Tennessee was already a successful playwright when they met, he became part of what was then called the "jet set" over the following years. Traveling and partying, drugs and alcohol, became his life. Frank, on the other hand, wanted a stable relationship and homelife with the man he loved.

The drugs caused Williams to become increasingly paranoid, accusing Frank of trying to poison him and even somehow causing Tennessee's bulldog to bite him so viciously that he spent several days in the hospital.

Williams told an interviewer at the time that "Miltowns (a popular tranquilizer), liquor, and swimming" were the only

Frank (left) and Tennessee in front of their Duncan Street home in Key West.

things that kept him going. His wealth could also now buy many of the benefits that Frank had been providing.

They started spending more and more time apart, and eventually broke up in 1961. Then Merlo was diagnosed with lung cancer in 1962. Although Tennessee was attentive for most of the time Frank was getting progressively worse, near the end he only came to visit hours before his death. Frank Merlo, "Little Horse" as Tennessee called him, died on September 21, 1963. His last words to Williams while they were alone in his hospital room were "I've grown used to you."

After Merlo's death, Tennessee became overwhelmed with regret and entered a long period of depression. Although he wrote critically acclaimed plays while with Merlo, none of his later work was comparable.

SAL SALINERO

Sal Salinero was a 4th generation Conch and Army Green Beret veteran. He was also an artist, self-taught since childhood. Sal spent most of his Green Beret days in the jungles of Panama in the 1960s. After getting back to Key West, he filled his paintings with the jungle foliage and colorful flowers, parrots and flamingos from his memories of Panama.

Sal was a prolific painter, completing upwards of 200 works a year, and was widely collected. Curiously, he discovered later in life that he was color-blind to green; yet the radiant, deep greens of his paintings were remarkable.

Sal was also active in the Key West arts community as a gallery manager at both the Key West Art Center and, later, Gingerbread Square Gallery.

He and his partner Jeff Birn met at The Monster disco on Front Street in 1982 and were together until Sal's death in 2015. His burial in Key West Cemetery included an honor guard salute by the U.S. Army Special Forces.

Idilio "Sal" Salinero at age 15 with his doubles
tennis partner Glenda Burke

HENRY FAULKNER

Henry Faulkner was an artist at the peak of his career in 1963 when he began spending every winter season in Key West. It was an annual habit he kept until his death in 1981. Henry was a close friend, and some say a one-time lover, of Tennessee Williams. That's probably one reason why he kept returning to Key West when winter closed in on his home in Kentucky.

But the other attraction the island held for him was that he could be his colorful, eccentric self and nobody minded too much. According to Charles House, in his biography *The Outrageous Life of Henry Faulkner*, he liked to ride his bike down Duval Street late at night singing the blues at the top of this lungs. "He was fey...why you can't be mad at a little leprechaun running around the streets," noted Margaret Foresman, editor of the *Key West Citizen* at the time.

He also performed in drag at Captain Tony's bar, back when it was a mixed straight/gay hangout. Straight guys loved him, according to Tony, and they would clap and yell for encores.

Henry Faulkner and Alice.

Henry took his pet goat Alice everywhere he went on the island, including to parties, where Alice's habit of slurping up cocktails from any glasses left within her reach was well known. But she would sniff the drink first, and her preference was Kentucky bourbon.

Henry brought a menagerie of other pets besides Alice with him when he drove down every year. Tennessee Williams noted in his book *Where I Live: Selected Essays* that "In winter, there is an explosion of the fantastic painter Henry Faulkner on the scene, never with less than a truckload of cats and dogs." He also liked to shout "Hello Girls!" out the car window as he passed a police car or fire station on the way down U.S. 1.

LEE DODÉ

Lee Dodé (pronounced dough-day) was a college humanities professor in Miami during 1950s, at a time when coming out as a gay man often ended a promising teaching career. He visited Key West regularly on weekends, found the freedom to be himself liberating, and moved to the island in 1960.

Lee was a long-time friend of Richard Heyman (later the mayor of Key West), dating back to their college days at Ohio State University. Eventually he convinced Rich to move down too. They starting investing and remodeling Key West properties together, although Lee repeated more often than necessary that "we were not lovers." It was an era when real estate was, by today's standards, dirt cheap.

He was an avid potter, served as director of the Key West Art and Historical Society for a while, and was chairman of the Old Island Restoration Board (forerunner of HARC) in the early 1980s.

Lee always added PhD after his name and, for awhile, also added a "z" at the end of it, out of frustration with how often the "é" was sometimes incorrectly pronounced, making his last name "dough-dee." Even more annoying, some thought his name was Lido Day.

He wrote two books later in life. One was called *Cruisin' Duval*, and it was a kind of rambling oral history of Key West. It was filled with tall tales of island characters and bizarre anecdotes, told like he was sitting next to you at the bar at happy hour. The book is a charming depiction of Key West in the mid-1990s, including a street-by-street listing of bars, restaurants, and landmarks—many of which are now long-gone. It is out-of-print and hard to find a used copy today.

Speaking of happy hour, his friends will tell you that Lee rarely missed it. And, if he was at his favorite outdoor bar at La-Te-Da, you could hear his loud, distinctive laugh from down the block.

The other book was unusual. It was entitled *Gay Happiness - How To Get It*. Although Lee lived alone all his life—and was proud of it—the book laid out advice and rules for finding and maintaining a gay relationship, all of which was annotated with extensive footnote references to psychological and scientific studies of the day.

✦ ✦ ✦ ✦ ✦ ✦ ✦

Air Sunshine served Key West in the 1970s and '80s, and called themselves "The Florida Keys Own Airline." Their ancient DC-3s felt like a step back in time and it was an ideal way to transition from the real world to Key West. Locals jokingly nicknamed the airline "Air Sometime" because the WWII era planes had frequent mechanical problems that caused flight delays. But Key West was "mañana island" back then, and promptness was not as important as it is today.

JACK BARON

Jack Baron did not start painting until he was 51 years old in 1977, after his lifelong partner, Bob Burton, gave him an acrylic paint set for his birthday. They had moved to Key West from New York City several years before and opened a small antique shop in Bahama Village. The shop window faced onto a bus stop where his neighbors, mostly black Key Westers, waited to catch the bus. He decided to try to capture the color and movement he saw outside his window every morning.

Jack worked in simple shapes of color, often outlined, and accented them with multicolor pointillist dots. He put his paintings out in the shop for sale, but there were no takers. Jack was having a good time with his new paint set, so he just kept painting more canvases.

Marion Stevens, a well-known local eccentric and subject of dozens of outlandish only-in-Key-West stories, visited his shop

Jack Baron with one of his paintings.

one afternoon and saw his orphan paintings stacked at the back wall. She loved them. Marion was the owner of Artists Unlimited gallery on Duval Street, and bought ten paintings on the spot for $100 a piece. She asked him to paint more so she could do a show at her gallery, which she grandly titled "A Star Is Born."

Marion was right: the show sold out. To be fair, this is not the story of a unschooled savant. Jack had previously worked in design and window display for Lord & Taylor and Macy's department stores. He just hadn't painted a canvas before.

Marion Stevens, sweeping the entry to Artists Unlimited.

Jack also started doing needlepoint tapestries, often with religious themes, such as "Adam and Eve in the Garden of Paradise." By the time he died in 2005, Jack Baron had produced over 2,000 works of art and was a bankable name for serious collectors.

✦ ✦ ✦ ✦ ✦ ✦ ✦

JOE LOWE

If you heard the sound of "Somewhere Over The Rainbow" or "Some Enchanted Evening" floating in the air as you walked down Duval Street in the 1990s, that was Joe Lowe playing his noontime "Music in Paradise" concert on the pipe organ at St. Paul's Episcopal Church.

Joe played popular music favorites and show tunes for about 40 minutes every weekday. At Christmas it was carols and holiday songs.

The St. Pauls organ is a beast: 40 ranks, 2,530 pipes, 5 divisions, 4 manuals, and 36 registers, built in 1923. With the doors and windows open in the church, the music ricocheted off the storefronts along Duval and echoed down the side streets.

St. Paul's church at the corner of Duval and Eaton.

Lowe was both the organist and choir director at St. Pauls for 43 years. He also moonlighted as a piano accompanist for singers playing at clubs around town. But his first love is religious music and he has arranged over 500 pieces of sacred music for organ, piano, four-hand piano, and chorus.

Joe and his partner, John Lyon, were together for 45 years. They met at a going-away party a mutual friend threw for John at the end of his Key West vacation. When Joe arrived for the party, he discovered that he was the only guest. Their friend was playing matchmaker.

St. Paul's organ.

RICK BERARD

Back in the 1970s and '80s, if you wanted to keep partying after the Key West gay bars closed at 4 am, you could head across the Cow Key bridge to the 24-hour Boca Chica Lounge on Stock Island. It was also the place where bartenders, taxi drivers, and other late night workers went for their early morning happy hour before heading home to bed.

Rick Berard was the owner and manager. The drinks were cheap, it was often mobbed from "last call" in Key West to past sunrise, and a DJ rocked the house beginning at midnight.

But the bar had a rough reputation. One local nickname for the place was "The Knife and Gun Club." According to former Monroe County sheriff Bob Peryam, "We were always the least armed people when we went there."

Rick thinks the bar's bad rap was undeserved. There were a few hostile drunks and fights back then, just like any Key West bar, but he says his slogan "THE NICEST BAR IN TOWN" was more accurate. It was on the sign out front for years.

Unfortunately, in 1989 several county commissioners decided to put an end to the few bars in the Keys with a 24-hour license. Despite plenty of opposition from Key West, their new law passed and it caused the Boca Chica Lounge to close forever shortly afterwards. Rick moved on, working his way up in the hotel industry at the Casa Marina and the Atlantic Shores resorts before heading north to Gainesville, where he lives today.

Boca Chica Lounge in the 1980s.

STEVEN TORRENCE

Steven Torrence was a good Catholic boy preparing to be a priest in his hometown of Seattle, Washington, when he did something odd: he started going to both mass and Metropolitan Community Church services. That went on for awhile until he realized that becoming an MCC minister was his true calling.

In 1985, he was sent to Key West for his first, and only, MCC church assignment. After 38 years, on and off, he retired in September, 2023.

The "on and off" part is because he resigned to become a Key West police officer for 12 years in 1999 and, of course, also served as chaplin for the police department. It was a little startling at first for church members to see him out of his clerical robes and tackling bad guys on the street in his police uniform.

Aaron Huntsman (left) and William Lee Jones reciting their wedding vows at 12:10 a.m. on January 6, 2015, with Rev. Steven Torrence officiating. Aaron and William were the plaintiffs in an ACLU lawsuit to declare the exclusion of homosexuals from the right to marry as unconstitutional. After several setbacks, they won. The ruling also meant that the ban on gay marriage that was approved by Florida voters in a referendum during the Anita Bryant anti-gay frenzy of the late 1970s was toast. They were the first gay marriage in the Florida Keys, ten minutes after the ban expired at midnight. Both were bartenders in Key West, and met at a Gay Pride celebration 11 years previous. Aaron was the reigning Mr. Pride.

During his years at MCC, Reverend Torrence married, buried, and baptized a lot of people. Steven was also one of the orignal organizers of AIDS Help, created the MCC "Cooking With Love" program to deliver healthy meals to people in need, and he still provides professional drug counseling.

Metropolitan Community Church, 1215 Petronia Street, formerly a Salvation Army Chapel, in 1990.

❖ ❖ ❖ ❖ ❖

Back in 1998, long before gay marriage became legal in Florida in 2015, the City of Key West enacted legislation for Domestic Partnerships. It was a well-intentioned measure to provide limited legal protections for the many gay couples in the city,

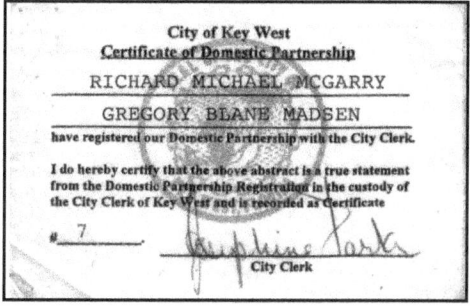

guaranteeing hospital visitation rights and the ability to make medical decisions for an incapacitated partner, along with funeral plans. But that was it. And it was only valid within the city.

Although lauded at the time as a big step forward in civil rights for gay men and women, it was not that popular. The authors waited a while before getting their Domestic Partnership, thinking they would avoid the rush. But when they applied a month later, they became Domestic Partnership number 7.

JERRY FRANTZ

"In the very beginning, Jerry was the only one that would visit AIDS patients. They would die in his arms," according to Steven Torrence, MCC Key West pastor. Hospitals at the time placed a "DO NOT ENTER - COMMUNICABLE DISEASE" warning sign on the door of an AIDS patient's room. "When the hospital would leave food in front of the door, he'd go in and help feed people. He would go to their homes and sit there and just be with them, so they wouldn't be alone, give them comfort and compassion, and fuss at them not to give up."

Jerry Frantz moved to Key West at the age of 70 in 1981. He had a lifelong habit of volunteering to assist whatever charity or person needed help. So he just continued, devoting his time to AIDS Help, the Key West Business Guild, Metropolitan Community Church, and other local charities. Jerry also sometimes provided a safe haven and father-figure for young gay men in distress in his home for the next 23 years, until shortly before his death at the age of 93 in 2005.

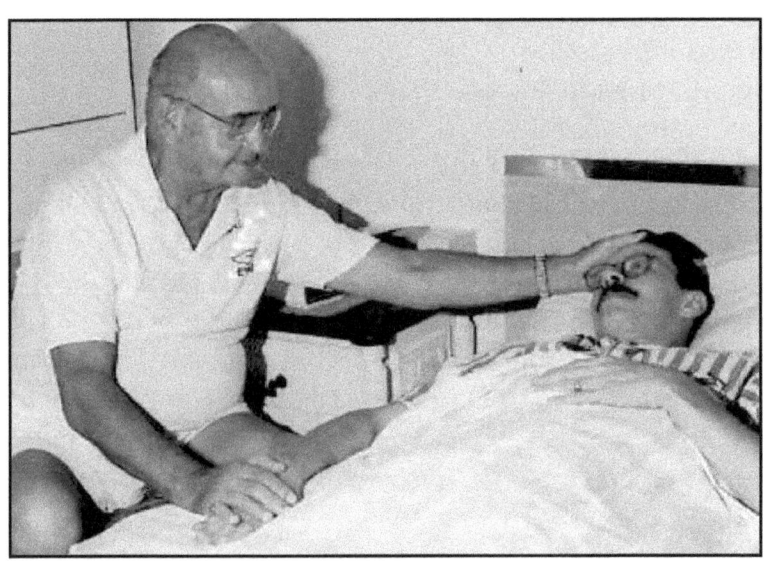

A True Buddy.

Jerry Frantz of Key West, Florida, is a true friend. At the age of 84, Jerry has been a volunteer Buddy to more than 25 people living with HIV/AIDS. As a Buddy, he provides reliable one-on-one companionship to those in need, many of whom have lost their income, home, friends and morale.

An inspiration at any age, Jerry brings support, hope and love to every life he touches. Miller recognizes Jerry and all the volunteers who dedicate themselves to the fight against AIDS.

Support your local AIDS organizations.

MILLER BREWING COMPANY

Miller Brewing Company is a proud sponsor of the Key West AIDS Memorial.

He was nicknamed "Mr. Fifty-Fifty," because Jerry was always just inside the door at Key West Business Guild meetings—sitting in his power chair in later years—selling 50-50 raffle tickets to raise money for AIDS Help. The Business Guild is the island's gay chamber of commerce.

He was an amiable but persistent arm-twister and, if you gave him a large bill for your raffle tickets, it might be tough to get change back. Everybody knew Jerry, and the top of his shiny bald head was recognizable in a crowd from across the room.

He accumulated plenty of recognition and plaques for his volunteer work, including being honored by the National AIDS Network in 1987 and the U.S. Surgeon General in Washington, D.C., on National AIDS day in 1991. Jerry was also crowned the 1991 Fantasy Fest King. But his favorite honor was Grand Marshal of the 2004 Gay Pride parade, just a few months before he died.

71

MICHAEL REECE

Michael Reece hitchhiked from Houston to a new life in Key West in 1976. That tall, blue-eyed, long-neck Texas boy was everybody's favorite DJ at the Monster, and later the Copa. He looked blissfully calm up on his platform at the corner of the dance floor as he cranked up the late-night dance tempo into a frenzy for all of us down below.

Michael loved his Conch cottage on Stump Lane, his partner Kenny Weschler, collecting McCoy pottery, and his garden. It was featured in the book *Key West Gardens And Their Stories*, by Janis Frawley-Holler.

Michael Reece, with his arms wrapped around Kenny Weschler.

An early morning fire of suspicious origin
destroyed the Copa Nightclub on August 3, 1995

RICHARD HEYMAN

Richard Heyman was tall and handsome, a former high school basketball player and owner of a chain of beauty salons in Ohio before moving to Key West in the 1960s.

He opened Gingerbread Square art gallery shortly after remodeling an abandoned grocery store at 903 Duval Street in the early 1970s. Richard painted the entire interior bright white, including the former walk-in freezer at the back of the space. It became a display room for erotic art. The massive door with a big latch handle was always left slightly ajar with a polite warning sign about what could be found inside.

Heyman ran for mayor in 1983, after being a city commissioner for one term. It was an ugly battle. His opponent, a Conch, tried to use the fact that he was a newcomer and a homosexual to scare voters. But Richard ran on a simple platform: the local utility services sucked and he promised to fix them. Water pressure was low and sometimes nonexistent, untreated sewage was being pumped into the ocean, and the local power plant belched fumes and black flakes of acid debris over the island when the breeze blew inland. He won, and became the first openly gay mayor in America.

June Keith was Richard's secretary while he was mayor and a long-time friend. She called him "Big Daddy" and included stories about him and his partner, the artist John Kiraly, in her book *Postcards From Paradise.* If you look carefully at the back wall of the set on a Golden Girls rerun, you'll see a framed print of one of John's tropical paintings.

Richard did not run for a second two-year term in 1985, saying that he hadn't realized how much work was involved in the supposedly part-time job. He had also developed a painful case of shingles, due partly to the stress of running city government. But by the following election in 1987 his supporters convinced him to do it again and he won a second time.

Key West City Clerk, Josephine Parker, administering the oath of office to Richard Heyman in front of the then-abandoned original city hall on Greene Street

Then, in 1994 Richard began to succumb to HIV-related illnesses. As the end approached, the city offered to honor him by naming a park or other public facility after him, and asked Richard what he preferred. He chose to have his name on the project of which he was most proud. The Richard A. Heyman Wastewater Treatment Plant on Fleming Key has since won numerous awards, including the 2012 Operational Performance Excellence Award from the Florida Water Environment Association.

J.T. THOMPSON

Key West has always been known as a live-and-let-live kind of island, where being different from mainstream American standards was tolerated—and often even celebrated. The local catch-phrase "Key West Normal" is a good example. But the 1990s was an era of especially divisive politics in America, with popular slogans like "God, Guns and Family" becoming a mantra for the religious right.

J.T. Thompson is a local gay rights activist that wanted to do something to reclaim the word "family" from being tied to exclusionary politics, and his quest was helped by being a graphic designer. He came up with the phrase "ONE HUMAN FAMILY" in 1999, then designed a deceptively simple black-and-white bumper sticker that he handed out free around the island.

Everyone in the world can share the "Official Philosophy of Key West, Florida"
ALL PEOPLE ARE CREATED EQUAL MEMBERS OF
ONE HUMAN FAMILY
Stickers are free • For more, send loose stamps & envelope to: P.O. Box 972, Key West, FL 33041 USA • OneHumanFamily.com

It was instantly popular, and requests for stickers started to come in from all around Florida, then across the United States. J.T. made them small enough to fit inside a regular business-size envelope. That facilitated the next phase of his campaign: offering free stickers to anyone that sent him a self-addressed, stamped envelope. Local groups staged fund raisers to support the expense of printing thousands more bumper stickers, and volunteers began helping with the mailing.

Today over three million stickers have been given away world-wide. And on October 17th, 2000, Mayor Jimmy Weekley made ONE HUMAN FAMILY the official philosophy of the City of Key West.

J.T. loves to tell the story of marching down Duval Street in full leather for the first Key West Gay Pride Parade in 1982. Today, more than 40 years later, he is still a passionate gay rights activist.

25th Anniversary Gay Pride Parade in 2007 on Duval Street

GILBERT BAKER

The rainbow flag, a cherished symbol of gay pride, was originally designed by Gilbert Baker in 1978 in San Francisco. He was asked by Harvey Milk to create a new, positive image to replace the pink triangle, which was originally used in Nazi Germany to identify gay inmates in concentration camps. Harvey was the California State Assemblyman famous as the first openly-gay politician elected in America, who was later murdered in a hate-crime by a fellow Assemblyman.

Fast forward to 2003, and Gilbert was looking for a way to celebrate the 25th anniversary of the rainbow flag's debut. He was impressed by Key West's recent adoption of "One Human Family" as the city's official motto, and had a vision of a 1.25-mile-long flag that would be unfurled down Duval Street from the Gulf of Mexico to the Atlantic Ocean.

So Gilbert contacted Heather Carruthers, a long-time Monroe County Commissioner and lesbian, along with Gregg McGraddy of the Key West Business Guild, and a plan was hatched. It would ultimately take Gilbert three months of non-stop planning and sewing in Key West, hundreds of hours of volunteer sewing help, thousands of yards of fabric, and then three thousand volunteers to unfurl and keep the finished three-ton flag aloft before it could be ceremoniously dipped in both the Atlantic and Gulf.

But they got it done, and everyone that was there to help with the unfurling during Key West PrideFest on June 15th, 2003, says it was an unforgettable experience.

The Sea-To-Sea Rainbow Flag, unfurled and viewed from the Atlantic Ocean end, on June 15, 2003.

However the unfurling was not the end of the story for the Sea-To-Sea Rainbow Flag. It was cut into about 100 numbered sections afterwards, which were given to Pride organizations around the globe for display at LGBTQ celebrations, memorials and events.

Section number 93 remained in Key West and a non-profit organization called "The Sacred Cloth Project" was formed to protect and share their piece of the historic flag. It has since been flown to Orlando and Colorado Springs for the memorial ceremonies for their nightclub shooting victims, displayed at the White House by request of President Obama, and traveled to Sydney, Australia for the world's largest annual Pride celebration, among many other stops. Section 93 was even reunited with four other sections of the flag (from Florida, Massachusetts, and Alabama) in Provincetown for a Gay Pride celebration in 2019. It continues to travel today to wherever the flag is requested.

DONIE LEE

Donald "Donie" Lee joined the Key West Police Department in 1994 and worked his way up to Chief by 2008. He is a fifth-generation Conch, and holds a degree in criminal justice from the University of Florida. Donie was also the city's first openly gay police chief. He retired in 2018, after 24 years of service. Donie's goal during his 10 years as Chief was to raise the professional standards and respect within the community for the  department. According to his friend and former fellow officer, Steven Torrence, he was always scrupulously honest and fair.

However, to say that the Key West Police Department has had a checkered past would be an understatement. It was notoriously corrupt for many years, and hit bottom in 1984 when it was declared a "criminal enterprise" after an FBI investigation. Multiple high-ranking officers, including the Deputy Police Chief, were arrested on federal charges of running a protection racket for cocaine smugglers.

Although the crime rate decreased significantly during Chief Lee's tenure, not all of his job was about fighting crime. He got one of his most unusual assignments just before Christmas in 2015. An anonymous donor gave the department $5,000 worth of $100 bills for a community give-back program. Donie had his officers pull over random Key Westers and, instead of a ticket, gave them a holiday card with a hundred-dollar bill inside, along with a message from the donor about appreciating law enforcement officers for the difficult and dangerous work they do.

Police Chief Donie Lee, Grand Marshal (right),
and Officer Steven Torrence marching in a
PrideFest parade.

JAMES MERRILL

Collecting seance messages from otherworldly spirits to write poetry might seem odd, but James Merrill did exactly that with the help of his partner, the poet David Jackson. The accumulation of years of ouija board seances at their home at 702 Elizabeth Street became part of *The Changing Light At Sandover*,

James Merrill (left) and David Jackson

his 560-page epic poem often described as apocalyptic. He later admitted to an interviewer that they did, however, interrupt their seances to answer the phone.

James Merrill is considered the foremost American poet of his era. His output was prodigious and he won just about every award that could be bestowed on a poet, including the Pulitzer Prize.

James' father was a founder of the Merrill Lynch stock brokerage, and a trust fund enabled him to pursue his creative life without money worries. He used part of that wealth to start a foundation to support the arts and literature during his lifetime, including hundreds of grants to promising writers, often anonymous.

Merrill also wrote a coming-of-age memoir, entitled *A Different Person*, about his travels and many love affairs as a young man. It is by turns comic and heart-breaking. "Freedom to be oneself is all very well," he once wrote. "The greater freedom is not to be oneself."

MICHAEL INGRAM

Michael Ingram closed his architectural practice in New Hampshire in 1990 at the age of 46 and moved to Key West. As a formerly married and recently "out" gay man, he wanted to slow down and enjoy his new life. So he bought Alexander's, a small gay guest house at 1118 Fleming Street, mainly just to keep himself occupied.

But a life of leisure didn't suit Michael and, before long, he both expanded Alexander's from 7 to 15 rooms and opened an architectural office on Whitehead Street to continue his career specialty of historic restoration. During the next 30 years Michael also devoted himself to the community, serving on the Key West Planning Board and Key West Business Guild, as well as HARC (the city's historic architectural review board) and the Tourist Development Council.

More recently, he acquired the Aqua Nightclub on Duval Street and remodeled the drag bar into Aquaplex, a dazzling, state-of-the-art drag entertainment complex with five separate venues. But his proudest achievement was designing and supervising the construction of the Key West AIDS Memorial at the foot of White Street on the Atlantic side.

Michael, when in professional mode, could be demanding and downright annoying at times. A good friend described him as "truly easy to love...but hard to like." He died in 2023 at the age of 79 and is missed by many in Key West.

HANNS EBENSTEN

If you happened to come upon a gentleman in a white linen suit, black tie, and straw hat walking around Old Town at midday in the 1980s, that would be Hanns Ebensten. It was his year-round uniform. He walked everywhere on the island and never owned a car.

Hanns lived in a Conch cottage on Peacon Lane with his life-long partner Brian Kenny from 1977 until his death in 2006. But he wasn't home much.

"Hanns' life was filled with caravans and train rides, charter planes and jungle safaris," according to an article by Daniel DiStasio in the *The Gay & Lesbian Review* of March/April 2008. "But it was also one of outrageous gay philandering and a penchant for tattooed men in torn jeans and uniforms. Hanns escorted royalty and tearoom queens, played bridge on the Orient Express and hanky-panky with guards in a Borneo zoo. But in the end, Hanns was both a perfect gentleman and the quintessential world explorer."

He is best-known as "the father of gay travel" for organizing the first travel tours for gay men in 1972. However, they were not for circuit-party types. The first one was river-rafting through the Grand Canyon. It was followed by explorations of Easter Island and the Amazon. Hanns was also a founding member of the International Gay and Lesbian Travel Association (IGLTA) in Key West in 1983.

He wrote eight books about his travel adventures over the years, including *Egypt in My Blood* and *Volleyball and the Cuna Indians*. However, the most interesting of them is *Pierced Hearts and True Love*, which explores his obsession with tattooed men around the world, published in 1954.

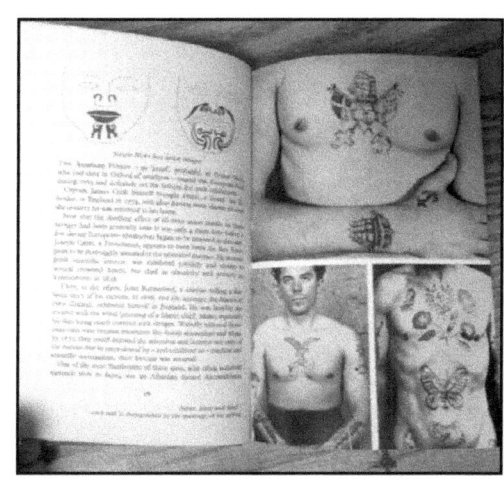

♦ ♦ ♦ ♦ ♦

Lighthouse Court, one of the oldest and most well-known gay guest houses, dropped it's "gay male only" status in 2015 and became "all welcome," continuing a trend that began in the early 2000s. At the peak in the 1990s, there were over 30 exclusively gay guest houses on the island, but only three were left in 2023. The popularity of guest houses with straight tourists and astounding rise in property values have been cited as the main reasons. The change typically happens when the property is sold to a new owner, often corporate, at a handsome profit.

BROOKS WHITE

Like many other gay men, Brooks White came to Key West in 1974 to reinvent himself. He went from consulting producer at CBS News Elections Unit in New York to commercial fisherman when he first got to town. But it wasn't long before he was back in politics.

Brooks became a charter member of the Key West Republicans Club and a candidate in multiple local elections in the 1980s, although he never won any of them. Then again, many public offices had never been won by a Republican in Monroe County's entire history at that time.

Brooks was much more successful when he switched to being a political consultant and supplier of campaign mailings, bumper stickers, and buttons. He was also a mathematical and computer whiz, and produced an annual Statistical Abstract to help investors spot emerging trends in Key West and Monroe County.

Key West politics was a no-holds-barred blood sport back then, and Brooks often complained publicly about opponents' last-minute dirty tricks—while being repeatedly accused of doing the same things for his own clients.

He is remembered today for the hundreds of hours he spent in later years creating and maintaining the first Key West AIDS Memorial website, adding the names of local victims as they accumulated to over a thousand, along with a photo and brief life story page for many of them.

Unfortunately, Brooks took his own life at his home on Catherine Street, while in the terminal stage of HIV-infection, on September 3, 2011.

TOM OOSTERHOUDT

He was called the "Colorful Commish," a nickname Tom Oosterhoudt acquired while serving as a Key West City Commissioner from 1999 to 2005. Colorful and "gay as a goose," as he once described himself to a newspaper reporter.

Tom also ran "Pelican Poop," an island gift shop on the ground floor of Casa Antigua at 314 Simonton Street. The historic former Ford dealership and hotel was where Hemingway stayed on his first trip to Key West, while he finished the manuscript for *A Farewell To Arms* in 1928.

The building had a fire in 1975, and sat empty for several years, until his parents bought and renovated it into a private home. Dad left the worst burned-out section as a three-story, open-air interior atrium filled with tropical plants, and turned the old cistern into a swimming pool.

Tom was famous for his holiday parties at Casa Antigua, his generosity at local fundraisers for the arts, and *Conch Color*— his magazine that covered local society happenings.

He was also a celebrity hound, surrounded in his home office by over a hundred framed photos of himself with visiting celebrities. If you were famous and came to Key West, it's likely that Tom finagled a photo op with you, often with a freshly printed "Honorary Conch" certificate as bait.

✦ ✦ ✦ ✦ ✦

PETER ARNOW

"The Key West Business Guild was formed in 1975 after a group of businessmen applied to the Chamber of Commerce to form a separate division for gay guest houses," according to Peter Arnow, the Guild's resident Historian. "And they were turned down."

So they formed their own. It is the oldest gay chamber of commerce in America. The Guild is now as large and more active than the local chamber, and brings significantly more dollars into the Key West economy with major annual events like Fantasy Fest at Halloween and the Red Shoe Drop on New Year's Eve. Over a quarter-million gay men and women visit Key West each year.

Peter has organized the Headdress Ball during Fantasy Fest each year since 1992. It raises money to promote Key West as a tourist destination across the U.S. He is also the Guild's Community Liason. Mr. Arnow was honored with a "Peter Arnow Day" by the Key West City Commission in 2022 for his work in the community.

Erica Rachel, winner of the 40th Anniversary Headdress Ball contest in 2022.

SUSHI

Every New Year's Eve at a few minutes before midnight from 1997 to 2022, drag queen Sushi (aka Gary Marion) slipped into a giant red fiberglass high heel shoe hanging off the balcony of the Bourbon Street Pub. As the countdown to the new year began, she was slowly dropped, touching down at Duval Street, surrounded by her thousands of screaming fans below, at exactly midnight.

It all started as a campy riff on the famous ball-drop in Times Square, but became an international pheomenom when host Anderson Cooper featured Sushi in a CNN New Year's Eve coundown show. Video excerpts from the "Red Shoe Drop" are now televised on CNN each New Year's Eve.

Sushi officially retired from the shoe drop in 2023. As Queen Mother of her troupe at the New Orleans House Complex, she plans to select one of her talented children each year to step into her famous big shoe and take the drop.

JIM TUCCI

Is the Harry Truman Little White House in Key West really haunted? There were rumors of seances contacting ghosts and hearing footsteps across the empty second floor at night. The mysterious events had a long history, and some locals wouldn't even enter the house "because there's something funny about the place."

So Jim Tucci, along with two fellow *Key West Citizen* reporters, Wendy Tucker and Kathleen Hargreaves, decided to use their reporting skills and an open mind to find out. Kenny, the security guard, let them in on Saturday evening, April 30th, 1983, at 11 p.m. They brought a tape recorder, camera with high-speed film, Wendy's German Sheperd dog Tanya, and two hurricane lamps. They stayed until almost sunrise.

All three were sitting at the dining room table just before midnight when Jim made contact. He felt a presence in the room. "In trying to explain what I felt, I had to create a new word: 'see-feel,'" he wrote later. "I think it's a new, different sense which combines two other normal senses. It was seeing without really seeing, and feeling without really feeling. But the two, together, enable you to 'know' something. That may not make any sense, but it is the best explanation I can give."

Next, he had an overwhelming feeling they were being "invited" into the Florida Room. They moved, and that's where the presence made itself known. During the next few hours, Jim became a conduit between the other two reporters and the ghost. They asked questions and he answered for the ghost, sometimes in a curious voice. Sometimes he said the presence didn't answer a question, and instead just looked away.

That's also when Tanya the German Sheperd started to intermittently whimper and howl, while staring into empty spaces in the room. The girls thought it might be President Truman. "It's not Truman," Jim said. "It's someone else. Tom. He's a caretaker. I would say he has blue eyes. Light complected. Thinning hair. With a felt hat. He always wore it. The kind of hat that was popular in the '40s. It was his trademark. The president used to greet him every morning. 'Good morning, Tom.'"

Jim's connection ends at 2:35 a.m. He says he is exhausted and his head hurts. He lays down to "re-energize." At 5 a.m. they leave.

All three reporters' individual accounts of what they experienced that night were grouped together on a full page of the Sunday *Citizen* the following week. All three agreed on the details, but noted that they "tell their stories with no small amount of concern for their professional reputations."

At a normal newspaper, Jim might have been demoted to copy boy shortly after handing in his story. But it's Key West, and a few months later he was made Managing Editor.

Jim also loved gossip. As editor, on slow mornings "he used to shut the newsroom door, turn around to the staff and say 'Let's dish!,'" according to former *Citizen* reporter Wendy Nugent. Jim was editor for six years, until he retired in 1989 after learning that he was HIV-positive.

CALVIN KLEIN
and
ANGELO
DONGHIA

This home, at 712 Eaton Street, was originally built in 1885 by local grocer Richard Peacon. Charles "Sonny" McCoy and his wife Merili later raised their six children there in the mid-20th century. Both Sonny and Merili were well-known Keys politicians. He served as Key West Mayor from 1971 to 1981, and they took turns as Monroe County Commissioner after that.

But the home is known as the "Calvin Klein House" because the famous gay fashion designer owned it for several years in the 1980s—although it was gut-renovated in 1978 by another famous gay designer and owner, Angelo Donghia. The home's elegant style set the standard for future island renovations. Calvin paid just under a million dollars for Angelo's handiwork in 1981—a shocking, record price at the time, which was announced on the front page of the *Key West Citizen*. It's now hard to find any house in Key West for less than a million dollars.

Angelo Donghia died from HIV-related infection in 1985 and his name is engraved on the Key West AIDS Memorial.

An onslaught of dollar bills in all denominations, rubber-stamped "GAY MONEY" in red ink, appeared in Key West cash registers for a while in the late 1970s, to demonstrate gay purchasing power.

Clay McDaniel was the island's top-selling realtor in the 1970s and '80s. He loved Key West and found its rough edges back then part of the attraction.

Clay was once overheard casually suggesting to a realtor that was picking up a key to show one of his listings that "You might want to cover up the tenant's dildo collection on the dresser with a towel before you show the house."

Plus, he seemed to know everybody. If you gave him the name of any local gay man, Clay could tell you a charming—and sometimes risqué—story or two about him.

He and his partner, **Fred Cole**, were a study in opposites, but a long-time team in real estate and life. They often befriended newcomers and hosted them in their home. Tony Falcone remembers their early encouragement and support for him and Bill moving to the island.

Clay and Fred were also the first choice of the dozens of gay writers and artists that bought a Key West home back then. "Nobody makes a fuss over them or anything like that," he said in a *New York Times* interview in 1977. The locals were too busy boozing and partying, according to Clay. He counted 31 parties he had attended in the previous 60 days of winter high-season.

Jack Phillips and **Joe Trice** were Cracker boys from North Florida. They moved their land surveying business south to Key West in the 1960s, a place they found more hospitable to a gay couple. Jack and Joe kept a crew of six busy marking property lines, settling boundary disputes, and laying out subdivisions as far north as Islamorada, and were the only registered surveyors located in the Lower Keys for 25 years. Phillips and Trice Surveying's office was at 1204 Simonton Street, across from First State Bank.

Danny Stirrup was a good friend and convinced them to buy one of his Conch Grove cottages, where they became neighbors with now-legendary writers and artists. Joe liked to recount their good times partying with Tennessee Williams, and how much Tennessee liked his southern-fried chicken.

Lew Savini and **Dennis Crowley** were devoted members of Metropolitan Community Church Key West and well-known as the Dachshund Rescue Guys. They sometimes had up to a dozen abandoned doxies they were caring for in their home on Southard Street. The garden path that wound around their house was solidly edged on both sides with upside-down empty wine bottles. Lew was also an instructor for business courses at Florida Keys Community College for many years.

Dr. Jerome Covington is a primary care physician who has been serving Key West for over 25 years. He has 5-star reviews on medical websites and a long list of credentials and service awards. One state award he received in 2016 honored his service to Florida's underserved communities. To say that Dr. Covington is loved by his many patients would be an understatement. They are passionate about how wonderful and caring he is, and want to tell you their stories to prove it.

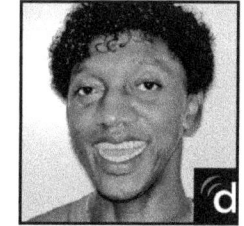

Jerome is also a big, tall, black queen with a sense of humor. The photo above is the one he uses for listings at websites that rate doctors, like U.S. News and World Report. And he looks good in both leather and drag; which, unfortunately, we hear he rarely does anymore.

✦ ✦ ✦ ✦ ✦

The highest point in Key West solares sh hill

✦ ✦ ✦ ✦ ✦

You would not have known **Leslie Mayberry** unless you worked behind the scenes at Key West gay bars and events.

He was the bookkeeper for the Monster Disco, and then at Atlantic Shores Resort for many years, along with helping out backstage for gay events. Leslie often brought his home-baked cookies for the crew, and loved to share the latest drag queen gossip—especially about Queen Mother DDT (David Thomas).

Gordon Ross has a daytime job at Island House Resort on the corner of Fleming and White Streets. But after hours he is a "production philanthropist," an unusual title which means he creates theatrical productions and events to raise money for worthy causes.

His most famous one, which he has been doing annually since 2001, is "Gordon Ross and Friends." Gordon is also a well-known Key West entertainer, both in and out of drag, and the event started because he and his friends were all performers, musicians, drag queens, you name it. They wanted to help local charities, especially AIDS Help, but didn't have any money to donate. So he created an annual pull-out-all-the-stops spectacular, with the best local talent performing for charity. The event always seems to have a few memorable surprises.

Gordon is also the author of *Key West - Dancing At The End Of The Rainbow*, a nostalgic look back at the 1970s and '80s nightclub and social scene.

Dennis Beaver started collecting Tennessee Williams memorabilia as a hobby shortly after Williams' death in 1983. It gradually became an obsession for him and his partner **Bert Whitt**. They decided to show off their growing collection at a birthday party for Bert in 2011. Shortly afterward, the Key West Art & Historical Society (KWAHS) asked them to lend it for an exhibition at the Customs House museum.

Dennis and Bert continued to expand their collection, and eventually it became a permanent exhibit at Conch house at 513 Truman Avenue. Then they merged with KWAHS in 2018. Today it is one of the most popular in the KWAHS group of museums around the island.

HELLO BIRD LOVERS
MY NAME IS FLAPJACK
I AM A ONE-YEAR-OLD
AFRICAN CONGO GREY.
THIS WEEK I AM
LEARNING TO SAY
I TAWT I TAW
A PUDDY TAT.
THANK YOU.

622

Front porches in Key West have always been a personal art form for their owners, but many were less formal years ago. This is one on Southard Street in the 1980s

Looking down Hunts Lane from Southard Street

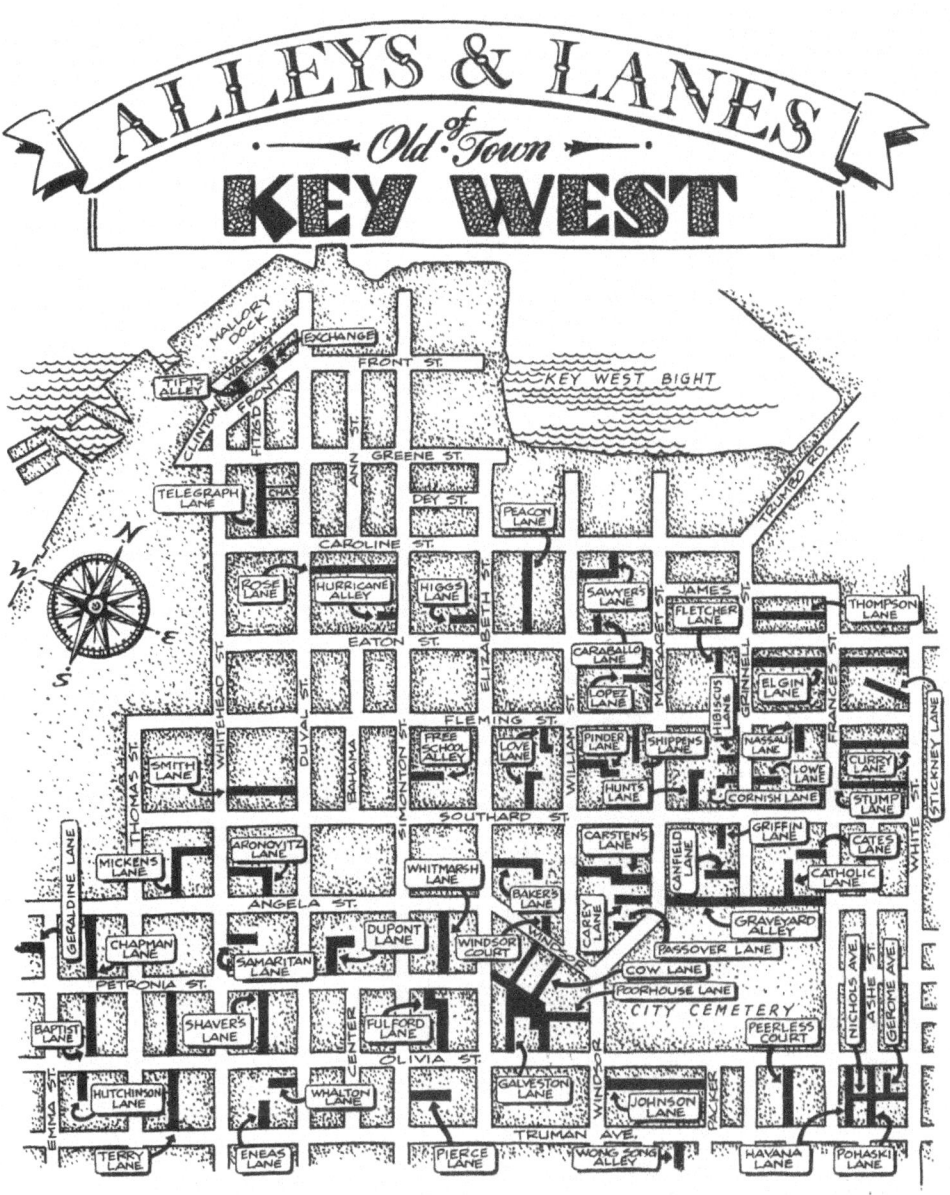

Unless you know where to find them, the narrow alleys and lanes of Old Town could be mistaken for a driveway and are easy to overlook. They are usually shaded by a tree canopy and quiet—except perhaps for the sound of chickens scratching in the dirt under a nearby bush. This map will help you explore them on a morning walk.

AFTERWORD

Life in Key West is punctuated with peculiar happenings. Because bizarre things occur regularly, their memory gets buried along with all the other ordinary day-to-day experiences—unless they are extremely weird.

But as the authors wrote this history and interviewed people who they knew from the last half of the 20th century, they started to recall almost-forgotten events that are truly strange by ordinary standards but not that shocking to Key Westers. The same thing happened to the long-time residents they interviewed.

One example would be a tale recollected by Tony Falcone of sitting on his usual stool at the U-shaped counter in Shorty's Diner on Duval Street, having breakfast one morning in the late 1970s. The door panels were pulled back so the front of the diner was open to the sidewalk.

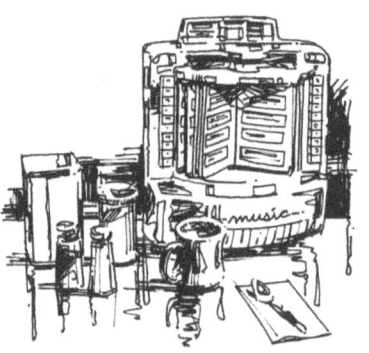

The sound of nearby screams made all the customers turn and look towards the street. A small man ran by, followed a few seconds later by his Amazon-size wife, waving a large knife and screaming obscenities at him. They were both naked. A group of diner customers, including Tony, decided to follow.

The husband ran down to the chain link fence at the foot of Duval by the Pier House and climbed gingerly over it to hide behind the storage tanks that were there at the time. As she got to the fence, the wife realized she had an audience. She turned and glared silently at the small crowd before stalking back down the street. The Shorty's customers went back to finish their breakfast.

If you lived in Old Town back then, you could easily guess who the pair was.

Slow afternoon at Shorty's Diner - R.M. McGarry

❖ ❖ ❖ ❖ ❖

We hope you enjoyed our collection of personal histories of gay Key Westers that, together, create a overview of island life and the evolution of gay rights during a bygone era. The unique, memorable gay men of future history are on the island right now. Please take the time to savor their company while they are still around.

- Richard McGarry and Greg Madsen

FURTHER READING

If you want to find out more about the gay history of Key West, here are a few suggested books and and a website to explore. Some of the books are out of print, but available from used booksellers online or from libraries.

Alarm in the Firehouse, by R. Kevin Mallinson (2021, R. Kevin Mallinson)

Key West - Dancing At The End Of The Rainbow, by Gordon Ross (2014, Lulu.com)

The Outrageous Life of Henry Faulkner, by Charles House (2005, Pub This Press)

Key West Sketchbook, by Richard M. McGarry (1990, Maupin House)

Key West Writers and Their Houses, by Lynn Mitsuko Kaufelt (1986, Pineapple Press)

The Kindness of Strangers - The Life of Tennessee Williams, by Donald Spoto (1985, Little, Brown & Co.)

Boy in the Sand: Casey Donovan All- American Sex Star, by Roger Edmondson (1998, Alyson Books)

Postcards from Paradise, by June Keith (1995, Palm Island Press)

Cruisin' Duval, by Lee Dodé (1998, Arete Publishing

Home at the End of the World, by Rita Troxel (2020, Pink Lightning Publishing/KMIM)

and

Solares Hill newspaper, from 1971 to 1997, in the digital archive at University of Florida library, accessible at: https://ufdc.ufl.edu/AA00031905/00001
It was a biweekly (sometimes weekly, sometimes skipped a few weeks) counterculture newspaper by local hippies, gays, and artists. The newspaper's articles, art, and ads give a wonderful feeling for what life in Key West was like in that era.

INDEX

Gingerbread Square Gallery
903 Duval
The Keys' Largest Gallery
Patio Sculpture Garden
'The Freezer' Gallery of Erotica
Pottery & Ceramics
Wednesday-Sunday   11 to 6

"...time past...has a lovely habit of remaining time present in Key West"
    - Tennessee Williams

www.ingramcontent.com/pod-product-compliance
Lightning Source LLC
Chambersburg PA
CBHW051542120626
46551CB00013B/1336